New and Selected Poems:

Bones Molder, Words Hold

by

Keith Moul

Copyright© 2021 Keith Moul
ISBN: 978-93-90601-59-2

First Edition: 2021
Rs. 200/-

Cyberwit.net
HIG 45 Kaushambi Kunj, Kalindipuram
Allahabad - 211011 (U.P.) India
http://www.cyberwit.net
Tel: +(91) 9415091004
E-mail: info@cyberwit.net

Printed at Thomson Press India Limited.

Acknowledgments

I am grateful to the publishers and editors who saw worth in the twisting history of many of these poems. Some have been revised and/or retitled more than once over their histories. I have selected some poems from my earlier books and chapbooks. I thank:

Red Ochre Review Chapbooks for *Beautiful Agitation*, editor Mimi Ferebee.

Broken Publications for *Reconsidered Light,* editor and publisher Jennifer-Crystal Johnson.

Finishing Line Press for *The Future as a Picnic Lunch* and *Investment in Idolatry*, editor and publisher Leah Maines.

Kelsay Books for *Naked among Possibilities* and *Not on any Map*, editor and publisher Karen Kelsay.

I am also particularly grateful to editors of the following journals for the day to day processing and selecting my poems from so many they are customarily offered for publication:

A Kind of a Hurricane Press/Without Words Anthology, Aji, Alliterati, Ann Arbor Review, Bacopa: a Literary Review, Burning Word, Cats with Thumbs, Chantarelle's Notebook, Circleshow: Seven Circles Press, Clarion, Collapsed Lexicon Anthology, Corium Magazine, Decanto Magazine, Delaware Literary Review, Divine Dirt Quarterly, Emprise Review, Eunoia Review, Folly, From the Green Horseshoe: Poems by James Dickey's Students; FU Review (Berlin), Galaxy: International Multidisciplinary Research Journal, Gyroscope Review, Hyacinths and Biscuits, Indiana Voice Journal, Inscape, LitBreak, Long Exposure, Mississippi Review, New York Quarterly, Noisy Water Anthology, Nthanda Review, Orbis, Pennsylvania Literary Journal, Phenomenal

Literature, PIF Magazine, Poetic Reflections at the Creekside Anthology, Poetry Superhighway, Pontoon Poetry, Pulsar Poetry Magazine, Quail Bell Magazine, Quay, Rainshadow Poetry Anthology, Red Wheelbarrow, Poetry Venture, Red Ochre Literary Magazine, Scarlet Leaf Review, Snow Monkey, Spilling Ink Review, Spring Lyric, Subliminal Interiors, The Ann Arbor Review, The Bitchin' Kitsch, The Cartier Street Review, The Centennial Review, The Criterion, The Hamilton Stone Review, The Legendary: Down and Dirty, The Literary Yard, The Mind(Less) Muse, The Mississippi Valley Review, The Pangolin Review, The Path, The Rusty Nail, The Scarlet Leaf Review, The Scrambler, The Smoking Poet, The Writing Disorder, Third Wednesday, Tidal Basin Review, Trillium Literary Journal, Two Cities Review, Vending Machine Press, Viral Cat, Visions with Voices, Wilderness House Literary Review, Wind Literary Journal.

Contents

Bones Molder

The Rise of Heat

The fire house, engine trucks, ladder
trucks, a happy, spotted dalmatian,
and public demand for first response
anoint the scene with immediacy.

The fireman is far away, however,
a black contingency of casualty,
the human intelligence cloaked in
the source and motives of incineration.

I infer his status: to remain, glossily
prepared, at hand within his edifice
until the flames threaten catastrophe;
only then, when air buckles perfectly,
spasms like an animal dies within it,
sparkling twists upward to the sun,
will this fireman choose to move.

Smoke and small fire mean no risk—
let rotten limbs be fuel, the infected
limbs be cauterized! A red beacon
his only pyrotechnics, he screams
and departs his sovereign station.

Reading German History

"Their job, as they saw it,
was not to question but to
blindly obey." p. 488

The Rise and Fall of the Third Reich,
by William L. Shirer

Some citizens have dreams: millions craved a Reich to last a
thousand years.
But poor of spirit and rich in hate, Hitler's people hauled a twelve
year caisson
to a continental mass grave. Some now, Hitler caricatures all,
seek more years.

My adventure began six months after the foul debacle in the
fuehrer's bunker.
Those who recall may crave easeful deaths or conceal them-
selves in doom.
Through most unnatural selection, "history" emerges as versions
winnow
politics, psychology and culture in dry spaces between the drops
of rain,
as "facts" loosed in nature to fight the motion of pebbles among
grains of sand.

Reading history, I grasp at pebbles, I reach into forgotten diaries
of genius
awaiting expectations; diaries of ordinary daily acts to live and
suppress the evil;

diaries of transparent extermination; forgotten dossiers with
helpless letters;
well-worn Baedekers routing travelers over streets and roads
that don't exist.

Too Remote for the Funeral, from the Podium

The dead never attend poetry readings but as shadows,
recognized only if expected to attend. You seem alive.
I come here to share my poems, hard as concrete, soft
as moss; empirical words, but not to wallow in memory
of this charismatic, loquacious boy I could not dismiss.

Well, heck: I once wrote "To a Friend Who Should Have
Died in 1965," to signal failure of our youthful aspirations.
Even now his artist's skills, mental athleticism, his humor,
(too often at my expense) arrest, but I felt he would return
much heightened by ex-patriot license recovered from ash.
He returned without joy, without stir, sadly without a word.

He had known, but withheld that we had not been friends;
that he matured before I quit adolescence. Now I admit my
pathetic ignorance shaped me as fifty years of distraction
intervened. Friends help through awkward times, depend
on us to do the same. My passport as a friend was stamped
"Canceled," my fifty years filled up my poems, I was alone.

But death backs in, a tandem semi, adroitly maneuvers in
articulated, deep diesel hums, to settle in torpid presence.

Universe of the Ants

(A ticklish tale)

After sixty minutes of *NOVA*,
my hide crawls with "social" aliens;
I hear enlightened voices from the past
proclaiming Man's divine descent; so
I call my helpful no-load broker
to buy more poison equities.

In truth, I know their feast day is near;
that an irreverent but consuming tide
will strip me naked to a pile of bones
with not a quark of grief as remnant.

I feel no terror for my billion-bite demise—

no, I often crave an imminent peace.

My terror lies with men sans me:
the leftover breed that continues
to read the bones of mammoths,
to read the glyphs of Man, but
born at best myopic, will not see
their noses for their faces,
their bosons for their baryons.

Augur of Winter at Home

Bones lie in mud; tendons strap their decay.
Live wings crowd gray skies with beats,
punishing crests of the dominant species.

The scrap for food occurs under trees
as rings accrete inside protective bark.
Cloudy-eyed insects burrow into leaf mold.

Curtain drains vein away under mounds.
Raindrops freshen shrubs like eyelashes
creating utter relief for a heated mind.

Missouri in Imagination

No morning or afternoon asserts its
command of light, merely the day
of orange glare that fills or empties
a passive atmosphere. Clouds form.

Stratus sky shapes could be ribs
as the blue ox *in medias res* fixed
to display its passing for loyal fans,
decomposing as a final act of myth.

Not sure, I wake with flat-sky mind.

Abandoning Hate

(a voice heard)

On your Harley there is the good wind and traffic, okay,
others with racy steel, but envious, laughable eyes.
Unless some asshole stops you, keep on going, circle
a wide arc, lay a little rubber, beam before the hot sun.
Stop for a cold beer, maybe two, let the sweat dry; think
of what you've known, what you haven't seen, here
in the liquid, glaring St. Louis landscape, city riven,
nigger swarms, nigger bustling, nigger nights burning
outside lonely doors, nigger vice, crazy nigger fucks, crazy.

You get beyond; a little woozy you sprawl beneath an oak;
you remember there was no time, even in the era of love,
that you were truly welcome in your own mind, no time
when you didn't crave gunfire and the smell of gunpowder.
Blood fixated you, seduced you to risk, floated your boat,
goaded your choice a blood-red Harley, crackle and fume.

Your sons knew all about it, almost without the need to say.
Your sons took mental notes, dated empathetic sweethearts,
married to build coalitions to resist in the neighborhood, more
than you had actually thought could be done. Now your sons
have returned to your circle of the wide arc with much to be done.

Anti-Allegory

Bald eagle pairs hunt from local trees all year. Now mid-winter,
I have seen no feasting, nor clean bones scattered carnally below.

One eagle squawks, herding prey within its mate's silent killing arc,
only to sweep the forest floor with wing-beats, to be secure and eat.
Or so I assume by their habits within compass of my home and trees.

With most Americans, I see them as symbols too, often circling near,
sharp-eyed predators with beak and talons ready to entitle our freedom
as portrayed by shafted arrows and olive branch: wingspread overreach.

Bones Piled by Oracles

As I pass them, people at work on scrub land wave to me.
My moving heart may be the day's only pause from labor.
Shiftless pioneers deposited their line in this blowing sand,
shaped them to protect the evil Gila, cactus, and salamander,
yet dishonored them with guilt for the buffalo's corruption.

Once far beyond their view, I wave back an ironic wave
barely involved in our shared humanity, mostly fatigued
after four hundred miles of the ever-persistent magpie.

The magpie speaks a I pass, nags of many pinch fist men
of the prairie schooners that jibe afore the scouring wind,
through dry washes, round a sand rock peak, aft the ghosts,
into one stony box after another, and when in sight of smoke,
fearing insanity, mumbling spit to the sun, croaking sighs
or catching paradise when they find bones piled by oracles.

An Archaeologist

See a graceful woman
in diaphanous dress,
at ease with her babies,
at ease in a time of empire.

Crisis erupts as lava pounds
from above, she drops her cup,
loses live touch of small fingers.

Dust and millennia smother tea,
ceramic shards, her garment
of oriental shine and complexity,
and the ever new alignment
of her family bones.

After Clearing Woods along the Fence Line

No complaints about high winter winds with consequences:
our maple scarred worse yet dignified more by its scars, but
so large to be isolated in place, with its fifty stout branches
escaping demise; maple aristocratic in more nurturing light.

I assume an easier generalship after tossing debris further off,
my frail fence relieved of weighty encumbrance, doe and fawn
nomads re-populating to wander, noses up, the ancestral trails.

A young man may kneel to his god to cheerfully clear his land.
I trekked to clean my forest space, left without a ready reserve.
I rest. More deer approach, alert yet absorbed in mystery, come
to sniff changes, poised with one foot in air as above a mine field.

I need not sleep, nor dream, nor read the leaves for auguries. My
own hand has written on a breeze my future, sweet as blackberry.

Crown of the Obtuse

(She talks first.)

We disagree and I doubt we can resolve it.
Our formulary offers no millimeter of antidote.
I detect nothing malignant in your tone of voice.

But our planets hurtle toward collision to hear
us speak: two spheres long synchronous conflict:
your truth would explode in my atmosphere;
my truth could poison an entire millennium.
Are we so mad for the crown of the obtuse?

(He finally talks.)

Anger passes. So, no, we do not go not mad.
Ideas held unblock and permit a fair sighting,
revive synapses long resident in our skies;
will deny us authoritarian prerogatives.
Our fools' faiths ignore our codes,
sprawl us groveling in triviality.

(He disowns his pride.)

I love you. I respect you. Permit me?

Do not misalign with those to whom respect
for me is unimportant. Our better angels
relent as well, welcome us; console us in
our single creed to dispute opinions fairly.

Breeze in a Hot Season

"This could not happen in ordinary circumstances"
said someone arriving at an extraordinary moment,
the kind from which birds and small animals depart
and a quivering sits on maple leaves in a hot season.

Breath told part of a story: rapid pants for oxygen,
most desert lungs, even in more complex phyla with
life experiences; each minute more stirring; caution
alters to panic, rare in forests, more common away.

Sirens force their howls, lights flash from the road,
chugs by vehicles redolent of sweet rescue; but their
crews seem bewildered by simple night and, toned
for immediate reaction, find no fire, find no mayhem,
find nothing at all unusual quivering in a hot season.

Dead Stalks

The soldier reticent from battle,
having served his chains
of command with distinction,
tells me he knows north,
he knows south, all coordinates
in fact, but he openly denies north;
would disconnect all ties to south;
shouts bloody enmity at east;

cannot avoid dead stalks
littering the west like corpses.

A Classic Chevy

An old man came to my door at an awkward time
for rekindling ancient friendships. He was as alert,
as I, but both mere shadows. He handed me
a 50-year-old photograph and said "I am Roy."
I recognized right now the 50 years ago boy,
I heard him laughing 50 years ago as if a joke
was happening this very moment, but for my life
I did not know Roy; I could only fizz a gape.

Both of us had for many years been beefy.
His lips now seemed incapable of joy.
My long hair concealed the barren spots.
His wife of forty years, whom I did not know,
had died in a crash of a '57 Chevrolet she loved.
He never had children. I have one daughter
who loves me even when I am so discomfited.

Roy would not step into my house, considering
my guests, acquaintances from my current life.
His promise not to let 50 years pass again
before we "get together" I took as a remark
that people make when strangers miss a joke:
men are not vessels for re-birthing memories.

Alternative Pornographies

What arouses our aversion excites us most.
Hate the paradox as we will, but revel in it:

when an arsonist perverts our loyalties, fire
consuming heirlooms; when vandals piss
on votive stones worn in honor of integrity;
when prurience is longing's only objective;
when to stain innocence nearing an insight;
or when love denies lovers to seek acclaim.

She may shrink back under tortured desire:
bullish with inevitability, he does not sense
her uncertain response, nor will his courage
be daunted as his loins engorge; each riots
over the frayed edges of their trust, slights
the other's tatterings, ascribes to appetite
his beefy mutterings, to dust her reason.

Will we condemn our common feelings?
Will bodies merely grunt with glazings,
grind into artful positions, or grovel at
a higher plateau of ecstasy (redundant,
monosyllabic, breathless, exhausted)?

If we *are* to be debauched, let the bodies
at least be slender, supple, and defined;
make them rippled in sinew, tawny, pert;

tender to arsonists no ambivalence about
combustibles, and eager for accelerant;

let our vandals be acclaimed for intellect,
let them prize the pain they spray about.

But keep our innocents pubescent, shield
them from casual ugliness - and especially,
ugliness that enjoys its pleasure; ugliness
still young, before profoundly more ugly;
ugliness that declares the spite of grace!

Encounter at the Cryptic Stone

Severe freeze relents as sun strafes over
our favorite limestone ridge. Our stroll
wedges into the resulting mild afternoon.

Windward edges coddle lingering snow
in their shade with no pose of resistance:
sorrowful old gods of sunless seasons.

We slow-walk beneath fossil-rich ridges
fearing faint risks over the cryptic stone
smoothed by glacier, yearning for spring
that may already be here. You let go in
a frolic between the line of sun and shade
portraying seasonal masks with your eyes:
first sorrow in dark shade then joy in sun.

A cold wind tumbles off a near brown hill
to chill the bone. I watch you and wonder
could life freeze us in intemperate divide,
you to toss in sunlight like a bobbing rose,
I to join ancient sediment, a strange fossil?

Beneath the Glare Are Ghosts

The desert shines as homage to sun,
dimming as rain dumps like baggage
on the platform of the ghost town depot.

Our arrival, on schedule, shivers studs
to greet us in memory of past hospitality.
Dark clouds blind us to our stinging eyes.

We must limit our stop to a fleeting chance
to meet a conqueror or pioneer who retains
the dying vision of a live town, ebullient
behind bent and rusted fenders, beneath
sun-yellow bursting flowers now emerged
after rain; the ghosts hearty and smiling;
not sere beneath sage in alkaline graves,
or diamonds of sweat sucking at throats
for gold hidden by fate, not to be found.

Great Falls in Summer
When Greatness Has Gone

Mama whirs like a hummingbird on the bank,
not with an abiding, tiny heart, but pizzicato flit,
pulse back and forth along the edge, capriccio,
lifted by a pounding heart as mamas should be.

Sonny sprawls obtusely by the Missouri's rise,
rushing silt back above the dam's mean whirl,
fertility lost to dark eddies, eddies swallowed
and tumbled upward by re-emerging spouters
more numbered than Sonny's progenitors tears.

What do next generations learn? Must they
risk their futures to footing on a muddy bank?
Will turbulence inspire their neophyte souls?
A mother expects more loss, no matter what.

Sonny goes a little dizzy, untutored in history:
the hot prairie air surrounds his head, the sun
dements his vision, the river beckons brown
and cool as escape seems only steps beyond.
Mandan chiefs and Lewis invigorate the spot.

Older sons quit the place. Mama had assented.
Sonny and siblings beheld the falls contained,
pleasure boats gliding on water calm as gauze.
Alarms may sound, crisis or test, echo off hills,
unheeded down stream where more local folks
devote their minds to new crafts' ill-fated design.

Commerce fuels hearts of manly boys, yet to go.
Mama's tantrums? Just talk. Mama's heartache?
Hysteria, more than likely. We'll seek adventure
for a wage, even wages of sin if the job is open.

A flood catapult that so intrigued dries to apathy.

Collecting the Senses

The high senses intercept
a barely perceptible sound—
water drips on a mute surface—
or is it blood's pulse in the eyelid
staying a while my eye's need to see?

I walk and sit on my low senses,
bottoms of feet and buttock.
Too long on the latter
makes the former tingle.

I haven't yet discovered mid-senses.

All this happens on an actual day, Tuesday.
I have saved the only known record.

Led to Slaughter, Chicago Style

"Modern travel: convenient speed":
Railroad Promotion latter 19th century.

Amid squeals cattle came along as well.
Destined to the center of stink, ever rising,
to be butchered, rendered down to hooves.

Miasma grew inland from Lake Michigan,
emitted constantly from the slaughterhouse,
miring to inertia even prophylactic minds—
miring stillness more quietly still, miring
moving ones to reckless speed—and more,
miring the lost to assume stink in themselves.

Often westerly, winds whistle off whitecaps
on track to open prairie, whether rime-laden
stink or the hot, humid malefaction on me.

Streets toss waste paper and cans; low chants
rise; drums beat to accelerating hearts, pedals
down start incessant whines; lips kiss ground
as necks bend in passion to revive the dead.

Piety gains no right with indifferent winds:
faith staunches not blood's vengeful essence.

Chance the passionless, takes no chance at all.
Its prehistoric, Chicago rituals do not surprise;
its olfactory mysteries (solved by nasal plugs);

its mastery of peoples' wills that lead like lambs
to slaughter: chance, the stubborn, noisome sow;
chance, mother to serendipitous causes, father
of obnoxious effects moves today's wind easterly.

A Non-Protest Seasonal Poem

The cafeteria cheers with holly, lights, children in good form. Mistletoe
would be too much in a public space, stolen kisses offending rectitude.
Jesus cashiered to do bank duty in the north with reindeer and St. Nick.

A veteran in old fatigues stands by, talking loudly to his dark reflection
in the window, or perhaps to others beyond the glass walking unaware
on the sidewalk. He derides his voice as only loud, not strong enough
for the fights he's set to in the past, or others he'll provoke now, so be it.

He displays no patch of rank or unit, nothing but the lost bearing of rank.

"Some officer," (to the air) "ordered me to see a doctor of disor-
dered minds."

Customers near dessert have reconsidered, left hurriedly by the side door.
Others make no progress, like hydraulic stampers without a wit to shape.
Faster now, ever faster, other military lower their heads to avoid his eye.

"I may have drunk kerosene from a drum." Then, more ambitious: in Iraq
"I know as a fact I swallowed fire from a buddy's helmet, then out of use,
but preferred to this civilian pap." Not a child by parents was left behind.

Outside, rain changes to snow. A festival of birth continues a
child's play.

"A puny voice makes a weapon of my words," he confides his
amusement.

Now a suddenly casual man struts toward the door, says "I won-
der," exiting,
"if you understand a Christmas blessing from a King now that you
hear it?"

Poinsettia, leaves lobed, bracts brilliant scarlet, sit on tables like pots
of blood.
Not the Mexican flower, not the laughs, not the lights, not our
veteran visitor,
not the snare we missed for kisses, not the everywhere holly, not
the indigestion,

but snow coming softly in blizzard drifts, make this stark story a
seasonal poem.

Plural Loneliness

Through years, each day this mailman
(unpaid) lay wreathes at lovers' feet—
sentimental offerings to pink,
washed feet, now past dancing.

For he never knew how to dance,
never sought that pleasure in whirls,
unless around romantic ideas of love,
not adept at happiness by force: he
was clever, true, but not so felicitous.

He had squandered early attempts at love:
over and over he could not achieve conclusion:
the loneliness (plural) of inadequate efforts,
the foul corruption of escaping gas, it seemed.

More aromas: all perfumed, stifled little sneezes.

> *There were engines stinking of fumes too*
> *(pall overwhelmed the entire track),*
> *the race was long, drivers rallied and fell back*
> *as the winner glistened leading the pack.*

Higher on Steptoe Butte: a True Possession

In spring not precarious, the old road circles up. I steer constant left,
quickly rising beyond the colonel's base perimeter, to hold my grip.
I gasp at oncoming views, jostled by ghosts from desperate moments
in the butte's history, troops outnumbered and taunted by tribes, buzz
of bullets presenting souls to Christ, collecting them as hills near dusk.
My emotions drift among shadowy undulations in the wheaten kingdom.

Clouds, I remember now, touch my face, drops condense down my
cheek.
This past was populated by desirous converting to righteous: life so short
such a rock would mark with graves a true possession, if tribes wiped out.
Bones decay, time comes round like the road, to sweeten consoling wheat.

That's my yarn, compelling me forward into intimate chance, rich in
both rue
and triumph, delights of others here to plot meridians, to linger in a trance,
to compose a chant, to adore finer distinctions that mere seconds can
create.

This fall chaff will gild the sky, swirling over and among harvesters' chugs,
the visible road a lace to tie Steptoe's hushed escape to his swelling myth
and Colonel Wright's knee-jerking vengeance to a policy of extermination.

After the Earthquake

Radical black scratchings mean Richter
has been alert. In spite of its sensitivity
you will not detect much obvious change
in property—broken panes, fissures in the
wall noticeable when expertly surveyed;
vertigo as you walk or while looking up.

One's heart cracks, but wills that it hold,
like ancient porcelain, its glaze sealing
the web of minor flaws. And the mind
exposes its casualty when a spider steps
precariously off its perch and flings its
essential being to float a web on breeze.

Sweet Chariot

sotto voce

I would not admit this to another soul
but I will to you, sleepless reader: I
need a ride home.

                    Too much,
much too much of a good thing!
On that road to death, low tones
accompany me, dulcet ditties echo;

since the realization of fallibility, as seen
on TV, I've been swingin, the choir's
been singin, the bell's been ringin,
the bee's been stingin and so on.

Keep it under your hat.

Waiting for a Headstone

A man came to my door
saying he had urgent words
to report from my father's grave.

I doubted his Missouri accent;
I suggested the hour was bad
for such talk; I hooked the latch and
told the man I couldn't see him;
I asked him to please go before
time's fervent spiral reversed.

For days I studied his departed face,
heard his lasting voice, felt the man's
movements and conjured facts from air
as if preparing to give testimony.

The man's presence compelled me most
during loud noises, bright lights, or riot
as if his purpose clarified in distraction,
or his core demanded peeling his flesh.

Cigarette smoke, beer, bleu cheese,
salty cashews and sliced tomato
in vinegar: many pungent, past odors
blew in the window; tastes
I wanted to lose had intensified;
flies buzzed suicidally at the screen.

My mother ignored time for two years
to buy a headstone, which cemetery
maintenance installed on a cold day
when funeral goers of my generation,
looking more back than forward,
sat lonely in colorless rooms,
speaking urgent, colorless words.

Reassembling the Bones

My air on prairie nights can quench a day's fire,
leave an ash to pollute a rising breeze, cause me
to forget the fiery sun that threatened immolation.
Weasels strew small mammal bones among clods.

Strength no longer returns each season, to plant,
to weed, to water, to reap and bale a harvest, so
these obligations pass to my sons, waiting eagerly,
and I venture into new dreams, severely confident
that the weasels will partner with me to collect and
reassemble small mammals for future dispatching.

An Early Disturbance Holds: the Prey's Agitated Edge

Fifty years past the shark, nary a sighting
on any of the world's beaches have I seen
another, dead or alive roiling the surf and
my excitable psyche.

                But I had seen then:
an elfin shark sinking with its own death,
like teeth, into the stormy Atlantic shore,
in Maine. I was twenty-one. Thrown at
me by the sea, its dissolute flesh sparkled
in the rain, on sand, gone a killer instinct,
yet still the source of a wind-flapping fin
and, at end, on hotter days that shine, the
reticular white bone. One infringement,
beautifully imaginary, through years that
both decorate and denigrate this vision
has kept alive a fear of violent intrusion:
rows of ever sharp white teeth churning
to violet the blood and flesh that violate
a privilege of the shark to kill, be killed,
and kill again, its obedience to predatory
death: this alone is the point at which we
touch, the agitated edge surrounding me.

Dakota Swim

Summer night here commands
our deepest dive, to fall foul of
air, so far adrift as we surface.

House lights sometimes focus,
but from light years in night's
pool, flicker like amiable stars:
but Dakota air douses each spark.

Or we see our own lights bounced
pathetically from aluminum cans,
or painfully out of prairie dog eyes.

Your silence comforts me. When I
blink, as I must, I miss you half-
seconds at a time: I strain to keep
you and the pulsing ocean in sight.

No landmarks loom up—
so we could be in a sea
with fish that always sleep.

Some artist showed deftness
painting a perfectly straight
and infinite yellow stripe.

Tolerating Fire

(the Chicago Riots, 1968)

Like a defiant stain our racial past
floats upward with smoke and flame,
a mural painted in immutable rust.

Savagery is a ditty so often reprised,
is a never surprising song and dance.
No human tragedy with fire neglects
the sky; nor do we, as afterwards
our eyes train on heat, to rise with it.

Cities may burn. Steel may stream.
Iron pipes from bygone time reduce
water to ironic trickles to extinguish
hearts and lungs simmering under
the crumbled bricks.
                          No one stands
to account for all the dust. And now,
after a few seasons with much rain,
the still sky rusts above ruins of no
remorse and intolerant of surprise.

Inevitable Winter

"I wish to smell ancient blood."

John Berryman

The shaken fence peels and sags;
the stones channel the latest rain;
heath returns to purple life;
corruption under bushes adds to soil.

An old believer in spring, I snag
plentiful firewood scattered about
and fill the barrow for more heat,
to prepare for inevitable winter.

At rest now, I question how much war
inhabits so many minds, how killing
offers the first option, how hearts
merely pump the last drops of doomed blood.

My fence requires maintenance to keep
out the deer and new holocausts; stones
mark millennia; heath clings to the hill,
softly, like the best infielders' hands.

For true horror, I read Berryman's life.

True horror demands injustice as a right,
the right of one blood or another
to be spilled, in spilling smelled;

the right carried forth from ancients
as though to smell blood on a rose
incites believers to action;
and the knife is to be kept at ready.

Mechanics Armed with Ancient Fire

Sleepless, I share my night
with soulless, tortured men
and tortured, soulful men
who plan my death
by righteous fire.

Never in daylight, never before
this time has this been clear to me.
The all-around-me world careened;
the all around me truth careened;
the all around me lies careened;
hawkers sweet on selling, sold
what ancient priests condemned,
what modern priests condemn
as heresy, urged on by ancient gods.

Ancient ideas inspire new work.
I had looked to night, my mind
wanting to move toward light, as
ideological soldiers, new mechanics, come,
armed to kill with new technologies.

The Road (One of Many Personal Freeways)

A BMW races by my old man's compact
4-cylinder, a young woman commanding
the road, the wind, her multi-hued scarf.

Apparently indifferent, affixing a stigma
to me and other defenseless drivers, she
enters her private freeway, private breeze
wafting her exciting personal hair; she
speaks privately into her personal phone.

My horsepower dwarfed, my ego tattered,
she vanishes among broken connections,
lost and found coincidences of travels.

College Basketball: National Championship Tournament

Since my high school playing days, March Madness
plagues me with its annual infection, true pathology
of heart-flow and respiration; a brain illness dreamed
about perfect execution by very tall robots in shorts.

Balls not only bounce, but careen from hand to floor,
arrant speed display, conditioning heroic to command,
total sight and encompass the entire rectangular court.

Players have defined muscles but their intellects know
entry into empty space to thrust through it in motion;
eyes connect within painted hardwood fields, bodies
move on goal, ever reducing visual expanse for hands'
frenzy and the hearts' belief. Then at the final buzzer,
when the O shudders to relinquish its defense and X
glows in its quixotic, crowning offense, is the game.

The Loss of First Occasions

I cached words before witnesses, both in
public and shadowy places. Today some
words seem sure based on my assessment.

Reliable as witnesses may be for their time
and place, many of them have gone, taking
their shares of assurance with them. Can I
be certain that real voices blessed real words,
or were caricatures in league with puppets
in the adventure of grand literary ambition?

Perry, Tom, David and Joan I hope were real.

Historiographers record faithfully the painful
births of poems, painful deaths of witnesses to
poems; ideas first chiseled in stone; fiery lava
erupted down a mountainside; stone wheels to
grind the wheat; prophets; royals, and warriors.

When I refashion phrases with more felicitous
words I am warmed, fed my bread, even ruled,
but do not prophesy, do not risk uncertain words;
I regret the loss of first occasions, those seconds
of only once events I miss, the enforced closing
of sympathetic eyes and ready, supportive ayes
that accompanied voices I did not figure to hear.

A New Intensity, Fire

"I was glad the colonel had quit talking about fire.
That had nothing to do with me."

Sergeant Muldrow
To the White Sea
by James Dickey

Fire on fuel feeds better igniting from outside to in;
catches its victim unaware of its preternatural speed.
Not talking now, the colonel's words echo in my brain.

Fire surrounds my escape, but so far igniting no flesh,
no tendon nor bone: never will my butt sizzle or pop
in fire's sling. Carnage may derange my war dreams,
sure, but my cortical neurons pulse coolly in obedience.

Others of my mess felt heat flare their fine hairs; saw
skin crack, curl; tasted death's entreaty in a dry mouth,
as fire followed in faith its only rules: fuel, oxygen and
a combustion source; speed to furnace heat; unerring
incineration of its object; and, if never confined,
destined to end its race as black, depleted breath.

For its light, alone first in speed through the universe,
this new intensity is now certain to power my sinews,
new life streams into my old synapses, forcing danger
and light to fill my mind, hurtling above fires of Tokyo,
as I steal my way toward salvation at magnetic north.

Experience at Lambert Field

No records survive.
Our pasts went by solely.
So many years have gone.

Like air above hot runways
his spirit memories sizzle;
as with oranges he squeezes
for his life sweet, sweet juice.

Talk has ended, leaving
vacuum pockets in air.
Absent time "explains"
echoes only he can hear.

Opportunities echo too off
the back wall of his cold cave
of speculation. Among people
she cannot redeem a moment
lost likely to excite disdain.

A hill crests.
Beyond waits a precipice.
Erect, he runs up to launch
with baggage filled with regret.

He plunges from experience
into history.

Matinée at the Eden Theater

Only John Wayne's heroics light the screen of the darkened theater.

Kids crowd the matinée to be noisy, free, thoughtless for Saturday,
ignore as faceted light bounces, squeals ricochet, John Wayne struts.

The projector ratchets to its stop: lyddite ignites to shine on Adam,
born here, now, his first moment in this theater's center; popcorn
and screen equidistant; God rips Adam sans umbilical from dream.

Naked, blind, Adam knows nothing but need: senses to see, to hear,
speak, eat, to speed encounter with Eve and Eden any way he can.

"I acknowledge my lineage from this miracle, my genesis from its light.
I deny any pretender's performance, as second fiddle, as never Adam."

"I am a man: born to covet, to possess, to arrest, to hold light as hostage;
own light for me alone. I refuse to bargain with God for control of light."

My senses return me as well to the world. I withhold belief. New Adam
may not exit the theater, with or without his protecting Duke, to the sun.
Eve, like blond Marilyn, so many blonds, slinks to Hitchcock memories.

At the door a serpent tears tickets: Flash Gordon precedes the next
dream.

Waiting for Secrets

Existence here mainly concerns survival.

Deep grooves through glassy soil mark
a road that proceeds behind a low hill
separating its object from the highway.

The grooves deepen over time. Trucks
or cars travel the road hill regularly and
return as often, careful to follow the ruts.
Tumbleweeds poise in the lee of the hill.

Nearby boulders look volcanic, explosion
following minor resistance, best spectacle.

Oil, gasoline, food and other necessities
may require fitness for a hundred mile trip;
willpower to supply a family with stores;
or refusal to succumb to a hot, dead place
that from the highway suggests pathology.

This country will not feed a herd; no rains
to quench a parch; not even seed revered
to plant or restrain chickens at the house.

The desert encroaches, remains. In winter
cold settles itself as a new ice age; darkness
comes early and stays long; days light an
unexpected universe; night touches directly
billions of agitated stars implying cataclysm.

So the scene spurs another Dante circle of
Hell, the damned expressionless proceed,
probably in a pick-up: a driver approaches
the road, the noise of tires crushing glass.

Although inadequate, a photograph can hint:
at this moment, children may be miles away
at school to learn secrets awaited at home.

Rain on a Grave

In his telling he filled gaps in true history with plausible stories;
often he wanted to stop, but struggled through peopled silences,
likely barring a force of ghosts from enlivening his private horrors
among his family. "Do not try to know my past" he seemed to say.

In six months, refusing food, rendered to 80 pounds from a stout 200,
he sagged to a final fetal mass and died, aged 67. I had no stomach
for his image like that. I missed his funeral. I missed his life entire.

Today I wake early; I hear commingled with the widening light of May
a steady thump of downpour; I make my peace with a northwest rain
that when I first arrived here would numb my brain for countless hours;
I exit a dream of rain pelting his grave: 2000 miles 20 years since death,
my recurring dream of rain on his grave is as close to home as I can get.

Words Hold

Child, Advice Once Perfect

when a living blue sky
        distracts your devotions

stifle pain that parts your lips
        pummel the ears
        thrash the eyes

you must
    reject learned display
           desire
the fire that bursts from the sparkling word

above a winter river oars glisten

an ancient man, wild in his heart

                stops to listen

Envy the Man on the Bremerton Ferry

I miss so much that time's vacuum ever grows
without strain like a black hole's event horizon.
Compared, my solitude evokes feeble words.

What remains to me are those random events:
check a need for friends; misdirect a stroll to
a run for one's life; strengthen my resolve post
trauma to rebuild life from unmet conditions;
surround myself with fruitful, not black space;
fail myself silently; course cosmic lives to meet
on ferries; give voice an object, time running on.

So, I am ready today to hear this fragile man talk
at me as though long absent, well-met, avuncular;
as though the ferry lounge were his parlor; the red
satin sunset his personal illumination; and I his shy,
intimate relative or friend, chosen to record in script
his painful tales and collaborate in his lost faculties
before the ultimate dark and stormy weather settle in.

Although bound for Bremerton, I am not his friend:
I occupy a threshold where needs his friend to be.

With his charming smile, he creates my convenience.
With his weakened eyes he readily obscures justice.
With some guilt common with strangers, I am contrite.

We head a stately progress until my silence, like space,
denies all my senses, drowns me in a basin still afloat.

Then his voice leverages my ease: I steal another's life,
my felony an act of uneasy and complicitous seduction.

His frankness frightens me. I am as timid as a swallow.
I shake in his reverend air. He blesses my belief, confers
ample commutation to fill a short trip. He strips my soul.

At other times, the *Yakima* would glide over Puget Sound
to calm my eddy in its wake, or else excite new fervor for
so many versions of waters. Not this time, with this man.

When finally I talk, my words invoke voices from below:
a stupid man who mumbles an inane homage to dinner
and freedom; a cornered man who stumbles, confesses to
imputed faults, not crimes, and anxious to achieve release;
and a man who shares his heart, as at home, or a friend's
parlor, freely comforted by age, with hurt, with empathy.

As he departs the vessel, the man on the Bremerton ferry,
I am changed, liberated to conjure a last assumption: warm
at home, he relaxes in his chair, grateful to meet his friend
to share a remaining moment of calm before lost to storm.

I return next day to Seattle, grateful to escape singularity
but not the old man's error, with envy for his friendships.

In the Air

Mozart might hold to my temple
an automatic gun to start crescendo
on my skull if his melody rang true.
Or, much less drama, tickle my neck
with a flintlock pistol to draw a baby
gurgle high up in the laughing zone.

Mozart, unlike any sound, any name.

Then back he comes, new and rich:
friendly sounds of complete accord,
with none of those jealousies
famous among woodwinds.

Funny that so many sounds fit,
so many fitting sounds, that place
doesn't enter into them; like an intruder
at the door, place comes with hard knuckles
banging; there is no need, here,
in the air, with Mozart.

Lovers

whether cool or mad
          naturally subtract the extraneous
          to get to an essential ease of position
          for their joyful, guttural utterances

eat at the same table, lie
          with fretful thoughts voiding sleep, swim
              against the same tides, laugh
at the expense of others, deny

conjectures of infidelity:
opportunities to self-instruct:
a predilection to self-destruct:
opportunities to others:
holocausts, perhaps.

If she sees coming
          any obligation
          a train
          reminder of old commitments,
       she would not be ready
             to oblige
             to board
             to put on a new face, to dress to seduce.

If after he delivers his message it is
          rejected
          ignored
          tacked on a bulletin board in a public place

he is unlikely to figure
    how to react to her refusals
    how to make his defense
    how to avoid places his name is known.

Each remembers dusky rooms
    filled with objects whose importance is lost
    that smell too much of the effort of loss
    that are not lighted to serve other purposes.

Nothing happed here except a brief try at pretend love.

Entitlement Lost

Hatethought cheapens all his days,
rock sharp, skinflinty, corrupted.

He stands borne by a wall flooded
by mindache and yet eyefishing in
shallows; while nutbearing,
or while yes yearning to
engage with pleasurebody.

Liege service empties out at pores.

Needles thread through holes,
but cease without firm seam.

Entitlement? 2-way lord-loyalty?
He desponds at winter rain;
he stands bereft in it alone.

Forced wandering dogs him
to search salve for bloody feet.

Beyond the Hunting Ground

A man came to my door
saying his stalk of a deer extended
well beyond the designated hunting ground
to end with me, on my ground.
"Are you aware of my deer?" he asked.

(I disdain the killing of deer
and rankled at his expectation
of advice to press his trespass.)

"No," I said, preparing to object,
but he promptly asked whether…
hunting had in pre-history
preceded mystery, that, of course,
hunters' need of food had preceded belief,
following immediately afterwards
the children's thanks for full stomachs.

Tracking deer or other game when hungry
became the adoration of many deities
for which hunters erected memorial stones,
near paths immemorial for pointed antlers.

To build my house, I cleared the land
of alder, cottonwood and fir,
revealing swathes of asphalt, rusted tools,
abandoned welds and windmill blades in piles.

Did believing hunters return to now my land,
rest, repeat their hunts, mark the generations
with full-bellied feasts of thanksgiving?

Due solely to this unexpected intrusion,
I reference this provenance in my pending sale.

Mathematics Problem #4

Mystic numerals mark my camera lens;
search unguided, but informed, the air;
extend my senses to find an accident
of vision. Perfect light floods Ianthe,
my daughter, from one side; separates
us only for an instant, but binds us
in a mystic force my aperture reveals:
she serves as scale for the beached
blue whale's jaw, blubber rotting.

Why connect in space and time; why
place my daughter in Behemoth's mouth;
why poise me ready in a depth of field?

Ianthe mugs with starfish, octopus, and
other salty denizens washed ashore, but
foresight I wish denies a Jonah residence.

I will never claim to equal Ansel Adams.

Solar right wizens the whale bone, and us.

Orange on the Table, Lights on the Hill

I forgot to take the orange on the table that you left for me.
My early hours make movement suspenseful: few lights;
colors mismatched, ill-conceived; socks mis-mated; yawns
every step from the cooling bed; shower; shoes at the door.

Then home before you, not having seen you, we had one call.
It's not really late yet. It's just quiet here, off the main roads.
The winter moon has now risen: it shimmers as frost crystals
illuminate hills, as sky blackens with silence of the universe.

I have not waited too long. You are not yet late, but I worry
that with slick roads some drivers may have appetite for risk.
And since your loving touch on my neck I know time empties,
that our mysteries, our intimacies, our mutual joy with words,
our mutual generosity to forgive our errors and cross purposes.

I shiver before our framed photos. I hear of tragedy's fallout.
I have known of cool compresses, bandages, even neoliberalism.
To walls I promise principled obedience. To pundits I will defer.
I start machines to fill the house with grindings and grumblings.

The orange squirts me as I see your car lights coming up the hill.

Join in Play

Past mid-night
Sylvia sleeps in the house
Rain thuds me out
Down the back steps
Insistent as a goblin
I wail away stagnation
Child memories emerge
Body-hankerings dismay old bones
Rain compels disbeliefs away
To the elation of thanksgiving
Two voices yell ascendancy
I hydroplane across grass
Sylvia joins me in play

Cat of My Heart

Cave drawings loom in my mind like a prehistoric moon on the horizon.
Elk, antlers bobbing shadows along the stone wall, flee; bears darkly use
distraction to slip by me to the blacker distances of the cave. I extend
my hand to receive as a gift the white featured moon rising out of reach.
This black spirit with white around her eyes steps into my history, easily.

Vixen, tempered female, damsel, mother to various litters from around,
tiny authority so in command of survivors Angst and Smudge, all fixed:
an earlier bunch, fluffed but too new for names, fed two eagles for a day.

Between cat feedings, fish-pungent as a salty shore, three jaws churning
as whiskers cake with carcass bits, my tame beast gulps cave air, always
shying from the blood smell, never rushing ready licks nor ripping to live.

Instinct wants a deep pulse, much more than I climb up into light to give.

Acorns of Consolation

Like a hardy and showy oak, my new guest
stood still in my living room; branched with
others, holding his drink convivially in hand;
to sway among the exigencies of others' time.

Perhaps his recollection was poor of stormy
conditions, youthful seasons of neglect, or
hopeful forest elections gone bad, and then
the promises a good tree needs gone worse.

Although he tried a creeper's length, others
crowded near his roots and claimed familiar
origins, genus, species totally in error, fauna
foreign and inferior from his careless words.

His defenses in nature did not include the lie,
so instinctively he argued evolution; a bearer
extraordinaire, he had hoisted loads openly
of dubious veracity and like a priest among
his flock, he dropped acorns of consolation.

Years after he had left the room, reports from
specialists in attendance, north pacific region
husbanders, that oaks reject moderate climate,
that offers to nurture would as a certainty have
been rejected. As if when we fail to recognize
humanity we commit exponential errors; plant
an oak in our plot the will to elect its nurturing.

Belligerent Action

Had sun shone on the fateful day, much would have been the same,
beyond peace keeper's control, but more people would check orchards
bursting with early regional fruits, spring rivers plunging to the valleys.
Not everyone saw, and few believed, the newspaper reporting of a war.

True to say, but aggressive war begins best in summer as commanders
consider convenience of attacking troops and temporary shock among
those peoples targeted for destruction. Later, these will be "good times,"
long days advancing without much resistance, lightning war, wildfires
of panic as the fifty millimeter leaves total separation in its bloody wake.

At headquarters, commanders scrutinize intelligence, offer calm assurance.
Armed forces always train to expert readiness. Rapid deployment, much
as
minutemen with muskets, instant mobilization relieves the worried citizens
of doubts regarding immediate total tactical invasion by land, air, or irony.

Militias not well-regulated retaliate by skirmishing along impromptu lines.
News arrives, is immediately touted from the capital. Citing provocation
and insolence among the people, the land army attacks on multiple fronts.

By a shivered wall a soldier stands hunched over, his eyes icy like yellow
tile.
The wall itself has erupted mortar, tips, and finally yields to early corruption.

What possessed supporters to lend their wills to misadventure? So
ardently?
To win this victory over neighbors who for centuries sang drinking songs,
woke up to labor in the fields, fish the streams, fix a clock, love their wives?

Beyond the wall, now powder, a teeter-totter hoists two children into smoke.
One brandishes a wooden sword, the other a toy rifle equipped with real bolt,
and they rise and fall and rise and fall, rise and fall as on a fiery white steed:
from ground atop the smoke to see the battle unfold in all the ruined acres.

Policies may change as leadership changes. Policing commences an occupancy.
Streets now broil with distrust. The old are worse for change; the young rearm.

Dress Warmly Still

33 degrees F. is the over night forecast.

Water and I near a time of cheerless solid.
Fine, that's scientifically predetermined.
I do not speak for water, anywhere or any
time. I will dress warmly and tell the truth.

Truth can be remote. I will go a distance,
(braving ice no price with my new scarf),
seek its rare beauty and its unknown ways.

If you please, come with me; dress warmly.
Your dormant garden reinvokes survival.
Shout praise for a walking stick; chant the
summer coming in, and *lhude sing cuccu!*

We usher in a cold dance and warm all day.
Observers note and commend our progress,
our cause being just, our pursuit perennial.

Bequest without Words

(Grampa August Uhl 1894-1982)
        (prior to 2016 Chicago Cubs' W.S. win)

Morning fills a packing box with doubts. **Gus, vigorous alive;
dead since '82**.

Memories attach to things: documented such as yellow snaps of
the family dead,
(tossed into the box); such as scribbles traumatic on calendar
notes (tossed into the box);
such as letters fleshed from my dreams or fancies (tossed with
contempt into the box);
**such as semi-pro ballplayer; such a story-teller; Gus
bequeathed no written words**.

I pack too what I must not discard: Gus' daybook of 1908:
Cardinals' and Browns'
season of box scores; topped with the Cubs' last world series win
against the Tigers.

My doubts concern my failed duty to him I cherished too late as
a fascinating man.
The trip was only a few miles by car, via I-70. We went every
week, or he and Reg
came to us. My opportunity to measure history was endless. I
goofed off instead.

Alders measure my years here; one dropped in my woods last
night, rotted, consumed

inside, as they will be. **Gus the doughboy sacrificed one eye to Black Jack in 1918.**
Fruitful seasons for peonies, roses and lilies measure Sylvia's years here, and so for me.
Recalcitrant land can be shaped and shifted, drained and pampered at physical cost:
land's scape measures our years here; land's character forces our obeisance no more.

One eye and all, Gus bowled and laughed all night with Reg, girls asleep in the back:
By '82 Gus simply could not make the call: his daughters grabbed his lowered flag:
Clara the bawdy; Marge (Mom) the stoic; Alice with a beer; Ginny, bawdier with 2.

I disdain what I cannot pack: punishing winter winds; a fence forcing deer from their trails;
sinewy blackberry twined with forbidding fruit; dogs whose howls rejoin coyotes' yelps;
eggs of slugs in unimaginable numbers clustered just beneath the cold ground's surface;
slugs in unimaginable numbers, twirling in wet like lotion, striking poses without bones;
slugs feasting on slugs in convulsing slime; slugs captured stone-hard by mid-morning light.

Who knew what steamfitters did, whether during or after the glorious age of steam?

Fortunately those things I cannot pack in easily cannot be abandoned: spring, summer breeze;
deer all around my fence eating tender shoots, doe and fawn

making do, but never a buck;
blackberry jam sweet with tang on English muffin; moving
coyotes yelp from all directions;
slugs, grand in ascendancy, slugs compelling icons of permanence
among gastropod mollusks.

**After Alice died young, the death march began: Reg,
Clara, Marge, then the wry Virginia.**

Sylvia awoke next to me, pronouncing new considerations of
bright and laughing possessions.
Apparently more packing boxes than expected will be needed.
But in sufficient volume and size.

Gus gave. Reg couldn't get enough, then passed it along in
levity to all the rest of us. **Gus took** decades of his many lives
from me: horseshoes tossed in celebration; ball played as wor-
ship;
beer in pails as neighborly rite most summer nights; ribs crispy
from the backyard fire pit;
patriotic songs as sung by doughboys over there, not by new
jingoes pumping breath for war;
to treat kids anywhere as friends; watching fish bubble in the
lake; to fish far from bubbles:
**Gus made me a man, accepted fondly my new wife; guided
me to fatherhood; seamlessly.**

This day I reach, now 68 myself, filling my boxes, my past is me,
my words are our futures.

My 70TH Year: Adventure in Abstraction

I get old. History tints my epiphanies more.
Like fingerprints, presences emerge, or DNA
stains the table top, the bedsheets and floor.
Maybe crime TV changes life in old age,
Not to arrest a felon, but to enjoy denouement.
I cartwheel to note the art of fine description.

Sixty-nine years of disbelief have disappeared,
often disfigured, into the past. My belief is new,
that any iota can evolve into my phallic totem,
my vaginal receptacle for unborn avatars.

A rose unfolds, canters in a breeze, strips
to its hip, joins the mulch, over time. Fact.

My regret longs for spring petals. Fact #2.
I have hope to see their rebirth. Too much fancy.

New buildings rise in promise, without deaths,
then accumulate the droppings as a favorite roost;
then manifests as icon of the past. Fact #3.

Time edges beyond my control. Fact #4.
Mine wandered off like an indifferent pet.

For fun, I photograph dilapidation. Fact #5;
Fantasy #2. Used structures; vehicles past use;
faces looking away, their holders unaware I spy;

the carcass wasting to its shining bones;
remnants not consumed by nature in its ardor.

I am left with only a warped idea of a thing,
or photo edited to show a new thing. Fact #6.

Photos omit putrid odors of the flesh, sleet sting
of Iowa winds, the bite but not the scar
of the nursing German Shepherd bitch. Facts #7-10.

If I am old, I am an old abstraction. Fantasy #3.
If, by standard of my time, I am not yet old,
aches comprise all my empirical facts. Fact #11.

Memories of my dead ache in few living hearts;
hearts typically deny my photos access.

My living complete my affections.
My dears complete the light of each new day.

YES, I affirm every motor in life malfunctions
with corrosion until it sputters and rusts away.

YES, my upbringing favored self-effacement.
Yes! I would not have it any other way.

Rain of Colorful Ribbons

I cannot see summer at night, but often
I cannot detect its essential soundings,
listening hard, then haunted, for hours.

Insects fall silent in rain that taps broad
leaves like Harlem drums of Chick Webb,
riffing toward a cow bell clap as he ups
the tempo ante to crescendo of the peal.

Chick sledges his hammer to the anvil
to ring as a torrent on the roof, through
overflowing drains, flushing windfall
into black ravines, to low wood edges:
black puddles rage there, at the edges.

Often I rouse from a jolting memory,
unrefined by dream, opaque, ugly,
clustered dryly with dull abstraction:
dull night sacrifice sans dreams' magic.

I may rise, I may dress, I may wander
into dark rooms, trailing echoes, listening
through stupid silence for Chick's joy:
rising to listen to night's silent terrors.

"Come down!" I shout. Sousa torrents
burst to bounding cadence, volleys of fire,
not military march but pitched operatic battle:
blood pictures, ribbons for sudden heroism.

Morning calm can multiply many delusions.

Avid Disinterest: the Yogi, the Mentor, the Model

A yogi relaxes, crosses his legs in an asana: he
tends to violence, but settles for mad oblivion.
Cautiously long ago he registered his madness.

A mentor gardener tests soil as if it is revealed:
she rests in epiphany that plants please her ego.
Also mad, her master credentials grace her wall.

A women models, affects that surliness of beauty.
She is a figment of her agent's fantasy and greed;
with angry pout she flirts with an aroused Nikon.

I ask no questions of the mad: yogi, mentor, model;
I deduce a bit of madness that yogi and mentor share,
Marquess of Queensberry fairness, observant of rule,
but no ropes hold our cravings for a blooded combat.

The model suits a pungent arena, divine, hot, buttery.

Poets' Memories of William Stafford

("Follow the golden thread")

Bill read to us in 1975, seemingly hours.

He projected each poem more comfortably
than the last. Not easy, but we held applause
as this genial poet massaged our discoveries.

"Poems must keep moving. Inside find gold,
follow the golden thread: you'll discover what
you know, as curiosity occurs, without help.
Never hurry. Warp and weave. Rely on knots
or tangles to change your way to each new line."

My home had been Missouri, but I knew Kansas
in Bill right away: his spare lips tugged at doubt;
oaks reaching up for oak space, prized on plains;
the yarns once heard he hammered into poems.

Kansas teaches us that pioneers survive: to talk
finespun talk; they talk straight talk with twists
skipping like dust devils over soil; they emerge
coolly from intense heat, warmly from deep cold;
that no rivers, even small rivers, begin in Kansas;
that moving by the great rivers cut edges deeply.
Like the rivers, Bill might reserve meandering
over his broad plain, to join his kind in muddy
deltas of plain truth. I was 29; stupid beside him.

Bill took my photograph, saying he collected images
of poets that he met. How could I believe that words
spoken by a poet reading poems could set my course
for life? I was afraid of fuzzy thoughts, not words;
afraid of minutes without anchor in empty spaces;
afraid to call myself a poet. When the photograph
arrived, he made me genuine. I had made a friend.

Bill lent his life to me, that part revealed in poems.
He would accept no tribute, but he would lead me.

Show me the golden thread, Jayhawker.

Silence of Sinews

Not at this time, but when still a boy,
did I often lift great weight to hurl in competition.
Such power was forfeit through time subsequent
to the press of blatant obsequies[1].

Some feathers, fallen as birds flew over, stood in for shot[2],
light but powerfully eloquent when put to use in flight.

And so through various times sinews, like a bole with rot,
endured the silence of atrophy, sinews drank the drunk of atrophy.

Time itself sat down wearily[3], the old visitor, often passing,
stopped by like a circuit rider, judgment at hand if all were ready,
but willing to move on quick-step if another moment elsewhere
offered vintage of stout heft[4] and a bouquet of amenable tang.

[1]No footnote explains life's obsequies.
[2]Think athletics, not cannon warfare.
[3]With its own obsequies no doubt.
[4]Judgment often craves reinforcement.

Down to Earth

A young girl, devilishly atip,
dances on thoroughbred feet,
like hooves, so lithe, so strong,
propelling her up, twisting her
sideways, rounding backwards
her hips into a joust of her joy.

She dangles her arms, tips her
head right before she strides at
the oncoming earth, her track.
Finally, politely, gravity applies.

Humility in Speech

I favor plain speech so
I don't covet reverence
accorded to divinities.

My work piles words in light,
fracturing and reassembling
meanings among inferences,
each word provoking reaction.

I ask easement through pain,
relaxation from tense ideas,
fearful tensions, tense
explorations, passport ready,
always greedy for simile,
but too humble for metaphor.

Independence Day, without License

Fireworks may fizzle their failure to light the path
but squeeze a button on annual rites of liberty,
often licentiousness in rowdy pursuit of rights;

Common Sense juiced rebellion's pain, fire-words
ignited the independence-minded: John Adams
loved his Abigail but sorely lusted for saltpeter.
Moderation (known as loyalty) sphinctered common
sense with detractors mourning their loss of income.

Breathe some gunpowder. Play at freedom in the park.
Appreciate soldiers or sailors, although often shattered,
for their re-entry into Hobbesian honeymoons belated.

You may hear gutter hearts thundering Mount Suribachi,
or old minds that curse above solemn oaths to the flag.

Or you may wonder at their plumped progeny, as beached
as whales, slobbering cheers from curbs at holiday parades.

I demand the freedom to muse, often far beyond license:
to pursue happiness while taking an inch, another there,
then a mile; without ever marching a foot toward risk
to defend, but never rushing to promote, freedom for all.

It's four o'clock local time. So far, no bulletins
announcing assassination, nor any attempts. Too light
for cowardice, too pleasant a day for ideologies
preaching annihilation or self-immolation. But

one more night of celebration, short moments really,
when the hot day finally cools way down –

the small and new ones shiver -

and patriots look for benefit in the general welfare.

Lives Want

"…month of the profoundest, ghastliest *solitude,*
in the midst of incessant talk and locomotion!"
    Carlyle in Germany researching for *Frederick the Great.*

Amid incessant silence and locomotion,
lives want explosions of talk: stillness
around edges of whirling is acceptable.

Many stifle tongues in ghastly loneliness
and fear, imprisoned by their rectitude.
Others shout riotous slogans, fear-filled,
want love, fierce leadership, and salvation.

Those who hate will be hated, whether
they pass to the front or guard the rear.
Carlyle forebodes no love for mankind.

Rending Mouths

The agitator rises before God
and the audience, performs
his cleansing without strings,
woodwinds or Brillo
and topples the house.

Upstaged, the comic, accustomed
to doing nothing, launches
off his edge profane missiles,
incendiary tracers, scatter-shot,
aiming to rend the trigger mouth
and other mouths to gurgle blood.

Eyes divert from the stage to train
on the blessed show back and forth.
Eyes tear in elation.
Voices scream "thumbs down!"
House spots dart at dark figures
like light sabers.

No Argument Rises

Iron-tinged landscape layers in insistence,
as if forced by heat to say "choose me."
I am rarely caught unresponsive, asleep,
gasping in the smeared red, even longing
for the cool blue rising in the background.

These rocks have been possessed by natural men,
pony-men always looking for, always finding
sun lighting their war. I cannot pioneer, I can
roar an echo over abandonment, or sit dejected
by the Gila's shape alive in an adopted hole.

"Valley of Fire"? No sane argument rises on wind,
no sere lip, raging blood or bubbled eye objects;
and all the bones (see the knees and elbows rising
from the sand?) eschew their tissue for mute stones.

The Arson Alternative

I worked late at the mind factory.
Being new to the work, I sought guidance.
The night shift resented my presence.

Bits of ideas arrived at the loading dock.
Shipping labels said clearly which side is up.
Some assembly seemed to be required.

Packaging materials seemed to me eloquent.
Talk in the rear warehouse went in tangents.
Motor carriers disclaimed any liability.

The later I worked, the more I appreciated
the irony; my boss had suggested, at first
at least, that I work only regular hours.

As pallets were stacked higher and higher,
I feared that new ideas were in danger;
that injuries caused may not be compensable.

I concluded:

work among ideas offered a precarious future;
the mind factory owner elevated profit
over knowledge; arson was a logical alternative.

Advice to Ripen Her Words

Reading no absolutist treatise has convinced her.

Days of relative good occur: no carpenter ants
in the sill; no too soft fruit on grocery shelves;
no June losing streak to end the pennant hope;
no overt faults crumbling at continental edges.

Bad or relatively bad days do occur more often:
some obviously false demagogic claims; friends
hoist on their own petard; innocence, some lost;
tragedy for people mainly fine, but unimportant.

At stake every day, good or bad, is self-respect.

She chooses a past time, not too early but fruit
still fresh, vegetables still crisp, resolution still
vivid as tri-color film. She wants a platform
to see what intervenes between then until now:
hail to fruits, hail to veggies, hail to vivid film,
but also sufficiently in charge to change her aim.

Yes, do not forget so lightly. Set a new parameter:
to define your scope; to know at law that police
rarely re-investigate former histories for suspects;
that whatever your wounding, you will heal; that
to influence the young, do not flaunt your whimsies
they will not grasp; conquer dialects, ripen words,
proceed within dialectics; planting requires nurturing
of a new tree; dare envision a bigger cosmic bang;

remember that, by regulation, auto underwriters
must ignore traffic citations older than three years.

If by this advice you flourish, and you are likely to,
pursuing biographers will drink much deeper later.

The Intersection: Birch Bay – Lynden Rd. at Stein Rd.

Unusually heavy winter rain sprays at
me from tires to obscure the road ahead
—at the turn, 5.3 more miles to home.

I rarely think of my mother, no need
(dead of her life of pain 9 years now),
and at this moment I must find my way.

I take special care at this dangerous time
as my father's lesson, whom my mother
(dead of her contempt 9 years now)
let float through his separate life, unmoored.

A sailor, scarred no doubt by war,
dad made it home to see me born.
He lovingly cradled both me and my mother
(dead of her loneliness 9 years now).
I keep the old pictures, recently digitized.

Under my own duress, still out in the cold,
yet comfortably sure of my way, my mother
(dead of her regret 9 years now) dissects into
countless drops of rain, countless moments
receding behind, countless caresses delayed.

As I age, previous generations all passed by;
I cannot re-capture the many crossroads; I

am lost to the black '51 Ford in which I learned
of stalls and ungenerous rust; I encounter
non-linear time, stormy discontinuity.

My mother (dead of her life's forfeitures,
dead of her weariness from life's omissions,
dead of her need for incomplete gaieties,
dead finally of time and her children's neglect)
is buried now closer to her husband than ever.

The Joyful News

A man came to my door
with news of joy in the neighborhood:
marriage to the west, birth to the east.

Harbingers had been known and especially good:
the marriage pressed through all contingencies;
the birth, although achieved, was hard.

The families have reappeared in the fields,
in the streets of the towns, repentant and pleased.
Celebration has been especially joyous for the faithful.

Such is the collective fear of alien ideas
that security forces have emerged theatrical,
as if friends of the bride just doing their jobs:
investigations have been aimed at merchants,
particularly those selling wedding gifts and baby clothes,

and, only through inference by some,
at our wider community.

Interior Design

My advice is:

exercise calms the mind;

go to your quietest room;
place a hand-wound clock
that ticks so to muffle
your beating heart
and ebbing breath.

This clock drums the tock of contradiction.

Then, discover there is no calm in you:
agitate contradictions in every thought.

I further advise:

that my first advice is unlikely to work;
that you get used to agitation;
that you be ready to grow old with it;
that you blend the décor with it
until the room, in times repeated,
compels your schizophrenia,
yet welcomes you both home.

The Western Desert

Paleface waves spilled their seed in sand,
laid rails in quicksand, then laid others
on red man ground. So many hustled their way
that the chiefs left me no permission in.

So I quail on its edges, always near the dusty road,
coming only lately, camping for beauty.

I am not fit for high climbing;
I am dehydrated with rank heat;
I circle the wrong circle
that might allow footing, my mind
swirls with my dust in air,
thoughts of loss
my only companion.

I rely on a dedicated cartographer.
I seek in the common past
to make loss my comfort.

But the chiefs have long memories;
they leave me not even a breath among them.

Sinew in Touch

At the pass overlook, a tradition of echoes
preceded my coming. I return for a recall
of my own voice from the past. Usually I
might hear a grunt at best, but this place
also interprets echoes, not like an ear but
a mind to consider anew my own sounds;
like fibrous sinew in touch with life's edge.

Other than milled boards and modern bolts,
no presence distracts from primeval marrow,
bones and stones erected to mark our eternity.

Now 72, my voice is clear; my mind is good.
I grunt. It returns sixfold. I grunt. It returns.
Fortune permits expiation and exoneration.

In Boots, I Defer

As winter passes, I get another chance.
Not the best, not my first, but a chance
you are willing to give me even though
I have yet to defer to the beauty of a rose
(what gardener may call my blind eye),
or derelict ignorance of its own root.

I wear knee boots. Sun means it.
Breeze shakes both sides of leaves
in piles: dead refuse of past seasons
and new mold urging rebirth in kind.

I aver that the plant itself prospers.
For now, gnarled by its own vigor,
the flower's fecundity terrorizes
the garden's needy spring time soil;
emits a sad confusion of the best,
a muddy soup anticipating summer.

I am no priest, no apologist, but
slog willingly toward *terra incognita.*

Voices in the Belfry

I held colloquy for many early years
with contrary shades of my own being;
pressed my beliefs, often heatedly; duly
paid or performed suitable penalties
when proved mistaken; hauled from
life's mine as penance metric tons of ore.

In fact, some arguments from either side
rang true. I acceded to honors bestowed
with a clumsy grace, no matter the side.
Most arguments floundered in superstition,
however when time advances its new rules.

Frankly, I neared eloquence. Not bad when
supporting epiphany, dimly lit, may collapse
under burden of those dependent on me too.

None may speak for pains unfelt. The scar
is authority for the lash. Piled dross recites
the purity of gold. Shaky and labored drafts
embed what worth accrues in the final poem.

I have a small hill. I like traveling long roads.
I have an ear for immaculate tone. But amid
designer disputes I have forged no golden bell,
nor consented to expenditures to make a belfry.

Past Understanding

I enter each new time, each new place
without preparation, without approval;
so I have exited an old time, an old place.

Regret for change is a cold mist,
also blown by winds, some trailing new adventure.

I wonder how to win my next match;
I will commit errors or misjudgments.
If too cautious, my support becomes smoke.

I want in my own life return privileges.

Why does the cartographer erase old testament?
I want new highways, spur roads and such,
but I want as much the evidence of history.
Must I recover old maps to find past understanding?
I have not forsaken even ordinary events
that I temporarily ignored; I want to mine
those private records, embellish them
with artifice, kneel before them as a votary.

So, now you grasp my problem.

Perhaps we share these thoughts,
perhaps we have wandered into new times,
new places without sufficient will
together, rarely considering old age
and thinking we'll be lions in loneliness.

True Irish Geometry

My welcome to this Irish pub is a Guinness in hand; more too as
hapless Yank
with inept step, aim, toss of dart: an amateur start. Welcome, a
very low score.
The circles' centers lure me, of course, to within their wire rings
but every dart
as if damned, turns hard to a joyless edge. No Irishman offers
more attention.
"Wind currents" enter my brain. Ignoring my doubts, I wet the
dart's feathers
and drenched in synchronicity, whistle one dead in the eye. The
game of life.

The Irish links test me too: touring remote rocks cruelly certain at
sea's edge.
Single lane roads twist through "real" wind with actual lift;
travelers entreat
rock deities—hilarity in this Irish pub rings hollow. I veil the
worst of jokes,
that Guinness will never be my drink, knowing well thus my game
is ended.

Dingle is a long way from Tipperary and Derry far still from
Marie's longing,
everything prejudged, loud but lonely, implacable places hemmed
by history:
all heart, all gospel truth moments before explosions, hilarity gone
in seconds.

You call my dart score bad luck. I say back that the earth tilts
toward sorrow;
that the dales hold indelible grudges; that darts cross a small
space of atrocity;
that pubs and all the drinks in Ireland tell a truth of lines compris-
ing geometry.

Your Flight Departs: Afterimage

The space you held so close
holds your face: fresh image,
your smile. But you are gone
with a white iris as paean to
our anthem. I delay going
for minutes of hot buzzes
in my ears, terminal noise
acute and low, thundering
engines roar at midday sun:

aircraft align and sizzle.

Columbia Gorge: Dirge

Reputed as a world wonder, the old gorge
of volcanic authenticity, whetted keenly
for geologic transgressors, river musicians
and wind surfers boring into upstream winds,

greets us with heat, 95°, and torpid, thick air.

We miss the adventure boat by a millennium;
we trudge to Hood River to pick wizened fruit,
(bings), burn as holy gifts to the alluring gorge,
air inverted with dog-day smoke and haze: we
"smile" at joy, "laugh" at miles, ill absent repose.

Birds scar every cherry swollen by rain, all hard,
all split. Often in the past we found mercy here:
welcoming orchards, terrain writ large on our map,
adored by locals who repeat their juicy gospels.

Although we still urge our dance of hot circles,
we gawk at other pickers of inferior preparation
and breeding who appear at orchard perimeters.
Laden with scavenged fruit abandoned to sere air,
yet needing ladders for height, at risk to rip down
branches, they swear like gluttons of sweetness
and drench with sweat to reach a heavenly prize.

At Some Distance, Fire

Without benefit of a sharp wit, sharp tongue,
he lagged through society's give and take;
he sometimes slowed, even paused behind
obstacles; he wondered if he would finally
be exposed once out the other side: later
in his life he accepted death as a true gift.

As his excitement built in coming to death,
he concluded all life a deceit; what others
felt must be painful accidents on the street;
that his children would, by inborn bequest,
suffer by freeze of distance from life's fire.

He was not young for death; he had faced
it when young and escaped with buoyancy
in the Pacific, both at the crest and trough.

But dread over time seemed to open doors
and windows onto death. A screen of death
surrounded each relationship. Tolls of death
were subtly exacted. Rewards to others who
seemed not freighted by death were tallied.

So, at some point, life having been learned,
he craved society with those dead walking.

As he assumed the fetal position, he refused
food, he abandoned intellect and empathy.
He may have thought, were higher authority
to intervene, to laugh at the supernatural joke.

The hours approaching cremation quieted him.

Trust in the Forecast

Eventually today's rain will come.
Each day contains the probability
at this season: wind adds to its sting.
We protect ourselves at our waking.

Weather known beforehand adds
bias to the wait: mind deceives
sense, predicting heresies; visions
foresee cheer, salves, balms
in the face of tornadic waste.

Personal histories caution a trust:
stay clear of the bending maple.
Place ripped boughs on the altar
of compost. Storm repairs ready
the house studs to resume shivers.

The house faces the truth: clouds
obscure; air lifts or suddenly drops
with humidity; as with fire,
with pain, our world sparks
only oblivion without trust.

Speak Softly, Carry
the Big-Leaf of a Maple

Others before me have detected
the impropriety and said nothing.

As they, I looked impertinently
close at big-leafed maple veins
like a layman invading privacy.

Some leaves fall early in response,
a brief, embarrassed pink without
assist of strong winds of October.
Those preceding me of ordinary
skill of observation have seen it.

But I learned something of flow in
tubed veins, trapped by membranes,
circulating through sunlight, a riot of
expectancy, a modicum of oxygen,
a growing excess of carbon dioxide.

A real scientist may offer a deduction:
not a theoretical, but real postulation;
no abstract epiphany, but a physical
tenet collecting from stars in a leaf.

I know also the risk of physical being:
that to breathe in is essential to my life;
yet if certain politics rises to ascendancy,
breathing out may be adjudicated a crime.

Without Perfidy

Under a rock ledge
near my house I detect
evidence of animal killings:
bones, skin, entrails of squirrels,
the skulls of frogs—
                              but no perfidy
as inferred when humans doubt
the felicity of their sacrifices
to gods and ancient orders.

Around the ledge is forest debris
ripped by recent high winds,
deposited for rapid decay
during another dark, mid-winter.

Above the ledge is soft, green moss,
tempting me to early sleep.

I have been my own priest for years.
My sermons are known for absence of protest.

Cowboy for Cars

No disrespect, but this peculiar salesman beckoned me.
Saw-toothed, twanging, he dripped down-home blood,
or rushed it, all flushing into his head at once. "Cowboy"
the name, livened him. He lived up to it, faced Seattle
car buyers eventually to find Nirvana on a thousand
range acres of Montana. So be it, but I was no buyer.

He intoned: "You can't settle for horse-life, saddled,
reined and spurred, poor as spit," "you hustle cars er
some such thing," these cars all badly used. "Jes settle
in like friens at a bar. You good folks and me'll get it done."

The cold night wind, Montanan wide, pushed me in then out,
a bellows of "love me, love my car" sucking air from my lungs,
both he and I white like glowing embers, like unshod steeds,
pawing and snorting to drive untethered to a big sky.
My evening wasn't wasted. Did I tell you I didn't buy?

With Camera in a New Neighborhood

Residents suspect strangers. Strangers lurk.

My pursuit of light could threaten security.

Here, ordinary presents sweeping pageant:
light attacks new obstacles: a furtive shot
clicks, I look away, lurking more than ever.

I capture light's puzzles as rain in waves
shatters to spectrum on sunlit windows.

East breeze ferries light drama to me:
flat light expands to rounded shadows;
blinding painted white of a church wall
of a minor sect shines as if combustible.

My accidental presence here has a cost:
a timeless day, my ready but imperfect
finger on the release; my ignorance, wet
and steadily pelted by eternal certainties.

Cloistered among narrow avenues, colorful
homes house a congregation, yearning for
salvation, eyes shut in homage to their God.

I do not expect an Old Testament flood.
Such beliefs merely temporize this light.
To ignore totally our formative history
would, however, be brazen. Clouds fired

in lightning like Yahweh on Mount Horeb
seduce me toward an exponential spirit.

History as I understand it, suggests love
as the guiding spirit of atmospheric light,
love here to merge its colors with a storm;
love, now fluent with light, could flourish.

Dartmouth, Eleanor, Beaver

Wind off Griffin's Wharf fills leagues
over the gray horizon. A winter storm
freezes Boston before a hot brew for
Christmas, all gratitude due to God.

The elements confront us; caution
as ever our watchword: deliberate
provocation fills fanatical air, threats
unite adherents to religious covenants.

Stately *Dartmouth* entered the inbound
tide first, her hopes unbound with her
bountiful cargo, rising too fully aware
that ambrosia comes to those who wait.

By the arrival of *Eleanor* and *Beaver*,
not ice but patriot ardor sealed the bay
against departure, all in limbo forbidding
negotiation. East India traders sailing on
American vessels, into American waters
with odds steered by recalcitrant natives.

Resenting the Senses

That movement beneath the trees
less than a minute ago has stopped.
Some rotting logs and shrubs quiet.
A soundless breeze mixes among them,
until sound rests throughout the world.

I have carried the scene as a memory
for twenty years; like a vole in my pocket,
it pops up, nibbles my shirt and my skin.
Perhaps I fell asleep under those trees,
perhaps I resented too much my senses,

until roots circled my head, my arms and legs,
trapped me as a beetle stopped on my eye,
acting predatory but so tickling my lashes and brow.

Those with faith in a future life must take pause,
to hear my story so bound in a repeated present.
I admit not looking forward. I see myself
as I was, furtive, perhaps conjuring a recurrence.